How the Sun Was Born

Como el Sol Nació

Willowisp Press®

Published by Willowisp Press, Inc.

801 94th Avenue North, St. Petersburg, Florida 33702

Copyright © 1993 by Willowisp Press, Inc.

Printed in the United States of America

2 4 6 8 10 9 7 5 3 1

ISBN 0-87406-649-2

How the Sun Was Born

Como el Sol Nació

Written and illustrated by third-grade art students of Drexel Elementary School in Tucson, Arizona: Francisco Arias, Martha Bojórquez, Sophia Campos, Iveth Chavez, Leo Corrales, Aaron Cornejo, Erisel Curiel, Claudia Duarte, Antonio Goodman, Angel Grado, Susana Luquez, Oscar Mange, Adriana Olivarez, Jesus Porras, Juan Carlos Rabago, Hiram Ramos, Sara Recinos, José Ruiz, Victor Salazar, Carina Silvas, Angel Soto, Jesus Valdez, Beatriz Valenzuela, Gabriel Vargas, and Brenda Vasquez.

Developed under the instruction of art teacher Nancy Murray.

Special thanks to:

Dora Recinos, for translating the story into Spanish; third-grade teacher Elizabeth Springs, for allowing extra time in her class for students to illustrate this book; and to Brad Curtis, Cathy Martinez, and Terry Romo for their help in typing the manuscript.

Dedicated to the students of Drexel Elementary School

Drexel Elementary School
Mission Statement

The mission of Drexel Elementary School, in partnership with parents, is to provide all students with the necessary academic, social, and citizenship skills needed to be successful at each succeeding level of their schooling.

The Story Behind the Story
of
HOW THE SUN WAS BORN

How the Sun Was Born was created by Drexel Elementary School's third-grade art students after they began studying ancient cultures of Mexico.

The illustrations were inspired by the yarn designs made by the Huichol Indians of Mexico. The story was influenced by the ancient Aztec idea of the sun having human and animal characteristics.

After hearing various stories of the Aztec sun, the students created their own story to explain the sun's existence.

Their story was selected as the Kids Are Authors™ winner from more than 560 entries in the 1992 competition.

La Historia Detrás de la Historia
de
COMO EL SOL NACIÓ

La historia *Como el Sol Nació* fué creada por estudiantes de arte en el tercer grado de la escuela elementaria Drexel después que empezaron a estudiar las culturas antiguas de México.

Las ilustraciones fueron inspiradas por los diseños de estambre hecho por los indios Huichol de México. La historia fué sugerida por la idea antigua de los Aztecas que el sol tiene características de humanos o de animales.

Los estudiantes, después de haber oído varias historias del sol Azteca, crearon su propia historia para explicar la existencia del sol.

Su historia fué seleccionada como la ganadora del concurso Kids Are Authors™ (Niños Son Autores) de entre 560 concursantes en la competencia del 1992.

Many many years ago a mother dinosaur laid five eggs.

Hace muchos, muchos años una mamá dinosauria puso cinco huevos.

SHE BURIED THEM IN
THE WARM SAND.

———————

ELLA LOS ENTERRÓ EN
LA ARENA TIBIA.

AFTER TEN DAYS THEY ALL HATCHED
EXCEPT ONE. THIS ONE STAYED
UNDER THE SAND.

———————————

*D*ESPUÉS DE DIEZ DÍAS TODOS
NACIERON CON LA EXCEPCION DE
UNO. ESTE SE QUEDÓ BAJO TIERRA.

VOLCANOS STARTED TO ERUPT.
THE RED HOT LAVA COVERED THE
LAND AND KILLED ALL THE
DINOSAURS.

———————————————

*L*OS VOLCANES EMPEZARÓN A
HACER ERUPCIÓN. LA ARDIENTE LAVA
ROJA CUBRIÓ LA TIERRA Y TODOS LOS
DINOSAURIOS MURIERON.

THE SAND IN THE EARTH BECAME HOTTER AND HOTTER.

———————————

LA ARENA EN LA TIERRA SE PUSO MÁS Y MÁS CALIENTE.

THE LONELY DINOSAUR EGG BECAME
VERY HOT AND IT HATCHED.
THE BABY DINOSAUR TURNED INTO
A BALL OF FIRE.

EL HUEVO SOLITARIO SE PUSO TAN
CALIENTE QUE SE ABRIÓ Y NACIÓ. EL
BEBÉ DINOSAURIO SE TRANSFORMÓ
EN UNA BOLA DE FUEGO.

THE HEAT FROM THE LAVA MADE IT GLIDE UP INTO THE SKY.

_____

EL CALOR DE LA LAVA LE HIZO QUE SE LEVANTARA HACIA AL CIELO.

THIS BECAME THE SUN.

ESTO SE CONVERTIÓ EN EL SOL.

AT NIGHT, WHEN IT IS DARK, IT
RETURNS TO ITS EGG UNDER
THE SAND. THIS IS HOW
THE SUN WAS BORN.

——————————————

EN LA NOCHE, CUANDO LA
OBSCURIDAD ENTRA, ÉL REGRESA A SU
HUEVO DEBAJO LA ARENA.
ESTO ES COMO EL SOL VINO A NACER.

Kids Are Authors™ Award Information

The SBF Teacher Support Foundation, formerly known as the SBF J. Hilbert Sapp Foundation, established the Kids Are Authors™ Competition to recognize young authors and illustrators, and encourage them to continue in their creative endeavors.

The Kids Are Authors™ Competition is a book-writing contest for groups of students from the United States and Canada. Entries are judged by a panel of professionals from the field of children's literature and each year the winning book is published.

For more information on the Kids Are Authors™ Competition write to:

In the U.S.A.,

SBF Services, Inc.
Kids Are Authors™ Competition
801 94th Avenue North
St. Petersburg, Florida 33702

In Canada,

Great Owl Book Fairs, Inc.
Kids Are Authors™ Competition
257 Finchdene Square, Unit 7
Scarborough, Ontario M1X 1B9

Winners in the annual
Kids Are Authors™ Competition

1992: *How the Sun Was Born* (U.S. winner) by third graders of Drexel Elementary School, Tucson, Arizona.
The Stars' Trip to Earth (Canadian winner) by eighth graders of Ecole Viscount Alexander, Winnipeg, Manitoba.

1991: *My Principal Lives Next Door!* by third graders of Sanibel Elementary School, Sanibel, Florida.
I Need a Hug! (Honor Book) by first graders of Clara Barton Elementary School, Bordentown, New Jersey.

1990: *There's a Cricket in the Library* by fifth graders of McKee Elementary School, Oakdale, Pennsylvania.

1989: *The Farmer's Huge Carrot* by kindergartners of Henry O. Tanner Kindergarten School, West Columbia, Texas.

1988: *Friendship for Three* by fourth graders of Samuel S. Nixon Elementary School, Carnegie, Pennsylvania.

1987: *A Caterpillar's Wish* by first graders of Alexander R. Shepherd School, Washington, D.C.

1986: *Looking for a Rainbow* by kindergartners of Paul Mort Elementary School, Tampa, Florida.